Book:
The Book

ANTHONY KAPFER

DEDICATION

This book is dedicated to all of my dedicated fans. Without your dedicated dedication, I would have nobody to dedicate this dedication section to.

I could also maybe dedicate it to my dead father, but that would make it a DEADication.

This page is blank!

CONTENTS

There is nothing on this page either

ACKNOWLEDGMENTS

I'd like to acknowledge that I don't know what to say here.

This isn't a good page for the first chapter

Chapter 1
ABOUT THE AUTHOR

It's unconventional to begin a book with the ABOUT THE AUTHOR section, but no one ever said books should be conventional—or maybe someone has said that. I really didn't bother checking. I just sort of wrote it, and now it's in a book. My book! Either way, this is how the book begins. Deal with it!

Who is Anthony Kapfer? He is a man. A man who lives life. A man who plays by his own rules. A man who likes to write about himself in the third person. Why does he speak about himself in the third person? Well, somebody has to.

The third person makes Anthony Kapfer sound important and powerful. It sounds like other people are saying great things about him. It doesn't sound at all like Anthony Kapfer is writing these words about himself while he sits on the couch in his underwear, eating half of a sandwich that he found in between the couch cushions. What kind of underwear do you think Anthony Kapfer wears, anyway? What kind of sandwich is he eating?

That's not important. What is important is Anthony Kapfer, the man, the legend.

The letters in Anthony Kapfer's name can be used to describe what an incredible and unique human being he is.

Awesome at being Anthony Kapfer
No one else can be Anthony Kapfer
The only Anthony Kapfer you need
Humble, modest, and also handsome
Oh boy, is he handsome, and modest
Never gives up, even when he should
Yawning as he writes this awful joke

Kontinuing on with this stupid bit
Are you kidding with that last one?
Please make it stop! It's too much!!!
For god's sake, why won't this stop?
Everyone probably stopped reading
Ready to move on soon. Ok, now!!!

Hello reader of this book! How are you? Don't answer the question, as this isn't a real conversation. Therefore, it would be nonsensical for you to start speaking back to a book. Unless you're reading this book in some kind of alternate universe where books are actually living breathing beings with the capability of communication. If that's the case, by all means, speak to the book. Get to know it. What are the book's likes and dislikes? Does it have any hobbies? You two will be spending some time together as you travel along through this literary journey you have before you.

In case you haven't noticed, this introduction has moved from the third person point of view to second person point of view, and it's counting down backwards to the first person. Isn't that exciting? Again, don't answer. If there are people around you, they will think you are insane. Then again, if you are talking back to a book, they might be right in thinking so. Either way, just play it cool. Even if you are insane, no one needs to know. Not just yet, anyway.

Hi. I am Anthony Kapfer, the author of this book. I have now begun writing in the first person point of view. I like it! There are lots of things I can say about myself in the first person. I can say, "My favorite color is green," or, "I have a recurring nightmare where I am minding my own business, and then out of nowhere, BAM! My head violently explodes! Most nights I wake up crying and in a cold sweat regretting every life decision I have ever made." See? Writing in the first person is great!

If you don't know who I am and you're wondering how to pronounce my last name (Kapfer), I will explain. It's pronounced phonetically. It's like if you took the word "Cap," and the word, "Fur," and put them next to each other, and then you spelled them both incorrectly, just to confuse people. Kapfer.

As a young child growing up, my classmates in school would sometimes make fun of my name. I heard it all, "Cat Fur," "Casper," "Crap Fur," "Crap Farm," "Monkey Fur" (that one was weird, but at least it was different), "Catastrofer," (I just made that one up).

What's your name? You can answer out loud if you want, but I probably won't hear you because you are most likely very far away from me. Or perhaps you're reading this book after I am dead.

If that's the case, I definitely won't hear you, unless I'm some kind of ghost and I happen to be haunting your house as you read my book. Wouldn't that be weird?

I bet at least a small percentage of you heard a strange sound as you read that last paragraph and are now convinced there is a ghost in the room with you. Don't be scared, I'm sure there's no ghost. BOO! Gotcha. Man, writing a book is fun.

I do appreciate you reading this far. In fact, if you were to stop reading right now, I would still consider this whole ordeal a success. But, I do hope you will continue to read on and enjoy all of the wonderful jokes, stories, drawings, poetry and whatever else I have prepared for you on this journey.

I am writing this introduction before writing any of the other content you will eventually read, so I will be just as surprised as you as to whether or not this book is any good.

Let's find out together!

Chapter 2
PRIVATE DICK EYE

I always wanted to be a private detective in the 1940s. That isn't possible, so I wrote this story instead. Take a journey with me back to the 1940s. It was a time when detectives detected. A time when they used words like "broad," and "dame," when speaking about women.

Actually, now that I think of it, the 1940s probably weren't that great. It's probably for the best I didn't live during that time, but let's read on, and see what it might have been like, had I been born in the early 1900s, or if I had access to a time machine. I hope you like this story!

PRIVATE DICK EYE

It was a night like any other night. I was in my office, drinking coffee. I wasn't planning on sleeping. I knew I would be up all night, crying a little, then giggling, then back to crying. That's when she walked in. She was very polite, and so was I. In fact, we still keep in touch. We are pen pals now. Her letters get me through the hard days, and those lonely, lonely nights.

Nobody ever said being a dick was easy, in fact, most of the time it's hard. Rock hard. But even though it's a rotten job, somebody's got to do it, and dagnabit, that somebody is me. Private Dick Eye. It's an unfortunate name, but I live with it.

Where was I? Oh yeah. There was a knock at my door. Then she walked in. She was a dame unlike any other I'd ever seen. With eyes in her ear holes, the body of a salamander, also she was thirty feet tall.

I'm being figurative here. What I mean to say is that she was U.G.L.Y. And I'm pretty sure she did not have an alibi. Oh if only that were true. If that were the case, I wouldn't have gotten involved in the tangled web I was about to be all mixed up in. In fact, she was beautiful. She was the kind of dame with long flowing hair coming right out of the top of her head, and eyes that could see right through to your soul. She had legs up to her waist, right where they ought to be.

She looked like she could have walked into any other detective's office in town, just by using the door. I was just glad she picked mine. But I kept my cool. I'd never let on that I had already begun naming our future children.

I didn't say anything about her appearance. I know sometimes broads can be sensitive about these types of things. And if there's one thing I am, it's polite to a broad's feelings.

She walked over to my desk and said, "I'm looking for Dick Eye. Can you help?" I said, "You certainly are, and yes I can. Private Dick Eye, at your service. And who might you be?" "Gertrude, pleasure to meet you," she said.

Her name was like music to my ears. The kind of music you make with nails and a chalkboard, but I didn't have the heart to tell her. What's in a name, anyway? It's just a bunch of letters arranged in an order that lets you easily pronounce them when you open your mouth.

Gertrude was the kind of dame that would tell you she loved you. Then when you pulled her in for the kiss, she'd stick the knife right in your back. Some guys are into that sort of thing. Me? I don't know what I'm into these days. Back then; I was willing to try anything.

Nothing could prepare me for what happened next. She began yelling like a baby on an airplane. Baby on an airplane? I can do better than that. Okay, I'll just keep going and I'll change that later.

The way she shouted profanity and racial slurs made this man sit up and take notice.

She had spunk. I told her, "You've got spunk." She said, "What's spunk?" I said, "Never mind that now, this conversation needs to help the story along, and right now you're moving it along about as well as a dead shark swims in the ocean." She said, "What are you talking about? I'm confused." I said, "We're all a little bit confused in this crazy topsy turvy world, sweetheart, welcome to the club. What brings you into my office tonight, of all nights?"

I opened the drawer of my desk and pulled out a bottle of Scotch and two glasses. I offered her one. "You got anything harder?" She asked. "Well I supposed I could try and freeze it, but I don't know if that will work. Not a big fan of liquids?" She shot me a smug look that hit me right across my face, as if to say, "I'm smugly looking at you right now."

I'm a man who can take a hint so I quickly changed the subject. "Did you know that it's actually the male sea horse that gives birth, not the female?" She looked at me and said, "What's that got to do with the price of tea in China?"
I said, "No, not 'tea,' 'sea.' 'Sea horses.' Never mind. Tell me why you're here."

She said there was someone she needed me to tail. I said, "You listen here, honey. I'm not putting no tail on no one. Not unless it's a drawing of a donkey's ass at a little kid's birthday party."

She said, "No, you idiot. I've got a job for you, but it might be dangerous." I said, "Lady, Danger is my middle name. Only it's spelled and pronounced Francis. Tell me about this little job of yours."

That's when she dropped it on me like a ton of bricks, but in a world where a ton of bricks is actually not a big deal.

"Follow my ex-husband around for a couple of days, will you? Then tell me what he's up to," she said. That, I could do. It seemed like easy money. Almost too easy. Definitely better than that thing about tails she was babbling about earlier.

"So who is this fella I'm going to be following around?" I said, trying to sound like I was asking a question about a case. "His name is Mugsy," she said. "Mugsy Hardknuckle."

She told me her old man was getting involved with some suspicious characters and she felt that her life could be in danger. I assured her that she was safe and I was the guy who was gonna keep it that way.

I told her as long as penguins fly high up in the sky, this ex-husband of hers wasn't going to touch a single hair on her body. She said, "Penguins don't fly." I said, "This guy is good. Maybe we should both get out of town for a while and wait for this whole thing to blow over."

I could tell by the way she said, "I'm disappointed in you," that she was disappointed in me. She said, "If you're too much of a chicken to take this case, I'll just have to take it elsewhere."

I said, "Hold on a minute there, sister. I've been called a lot of things by a dame. I've been called a jerk, a creep, a blowhard, a lint licker, a spunk bubble, a reptilian rabble rouser. I've been called inadequate, a coward, a man-child, a worthless husk of a man, but never a chicken. I'll take your case. What do I need to know about old Mugsy, anyway?"

She said, "All you need to know is that he's got a quick temper and an even quicker trigger finger." I said, "That sounds like a tongue twister to me. Try and say that five times fast." She said, "This is serious. You won't be saying

anything five times fast when you're six feet under."
"I'm not very good at math," I told her, "But what I am good at is taking down guys like Mugsy."

Just then, her ex-husband Mugsy busted through the door holding a pistol. I figured one of two things was happening: either he was a door-to-door revolver salesman, or my goose was cooked. I had just put the goose in the oven, not fifteen minutes ago, and I liked the meat a little bit well done, so that couldn't be it.

I quickly pulled out my .38 Special to show old Mugsy that I wasn't really in the market for a new gun. But like any good salesman, he didn't give up. He walked right over to me and shoved that thing right in my face. I think he was trying to show me how shiny and new it looked. I was certainly impressed.

"How much do you want for her?" I said, referring to the gun. "I'll take your life, then I'll take the girl," Mugsy said, referring to my life, and then Gertrude.

I realized he wasn't trying to sell me a revolver at all. I thought it was curtains for me. But no, my office had venetian blinds.

Just then, Gertrude picked up my bottle of Scotch and smashed it over Mugsy's head. He collapsed on the floor.

I looked her right in the eyes and said, "Hey, that was a 12 year old Scotch." She said, "Put it on my tab." And then walked right out of my office.

I sent her an invoice for the broken bottle of Scotch. I also wrote her a letter. It said, "Lady, I think you're a real swell gal. You saved my life back there, but you also saved my heart. How's about you and me go out for a drink some place, some time?"

She wrote me back a letter that said, "I just started sort of seeing someone. It's a little bit complicated, but I would totally be down to be friends. Maybe we can grab a cup of coffee or something?"

It starts with a cup of Joe and ends with a little bit of Dick. Private Dick Eye. Another case solved.

Chapter 3
PROFESSIONAL PARTY POOPER

Hi, my name is Alfonso. I am offering my unique, professional party services to you, at an unbeatable price. I'm available for all types of parties. Whether you're throwing a birthday party, an engagement party, bachelor party, bachelorette party, wedding reception, anniversary, bar mitzvah, bat mitzvah, baptism, or even a funeral reception, your party needs me!

For a nominal fee, I will show up, seemingly unexpected, and uninvited, to your party, and complain, insult, and attempt to ruin all the fun. By comparison, you will seem like the life of the party!

Just picture it. I walk into the room and immediately start complaining about the volume and quality of the music that is playing. I'll say something like, "Who is the DJ? This music is terrible. Does it have to be so loud? What kind of party is this?" I will really cause a scene. I'll start throwing things. I'll insult people. I'll even curl up in the fetal position and start sobbing uncontrollably. Everyone at the party will be staring right at me, thinking, "Oh no, this party is surely over." That's where you come in.

All you have to do is say, "Listen square, we all came here to party, and I happen to love this song. Now let's dance!" All of a sudden, everyone in the room is united, standing up against a common enemy: Me! Your party is instantly more fun than it was before I came in, pouting and whining and getting my tears all over the place.

My service is also perfect for very small, very private celebrations. Got a wedding anniversary coming up? Call me now! Men, impress your wives by hiring me to pretend to break into your home while you prepare your anniversary dinner. I will kick the door in, without warning, and start throwing ninja stars and doing roundhouse kicks at no one in particular. Then I'll go into the kitchen and knock over all the pots and pans on the stove, spilling all of the "food," you've prepared all over the floor. All you have to do is yell, "Get out of here now, or I'll hurt you real bad!" Then I'll run out the back door, into the night.

Your wife will be impressed by how well you protected your home and your family. Plus, you will have to order take out, since your dinner was ruined. Now she will never have to know just how terrible the meal you were preparing would have been. Anniversary saved!

Here's another scenario. Let's say a distant relative has died. Everyone is gathered around, paying respects, and exchanging memories. I come bursting into the room, and I'll say something like, "Who did the make up on this sorry excuse for a corpse? It looks like Bozo The Clown died and went to clown hell! And let's be honest, uncle Roy wasn't the nicest guy in the world. Aren't we all a little better off now that he isn't around?" Uh oh, who is going to step up and defend the memory and honor of poor old uncle Roy? YOU! That's who! You'll be an instant hit.

Hell, for an additional fee, you can even get physical with me. Grab me by the neck and throw me out the door. Yell something cool like, "And don't you come back now, you hear?" People will applaud, and cheer. They will raise you up on their shoulders and say, "Hip hip, hooray. Three cheers for you!" If uncle Roy wasn't so dead, he would probably high five you.

You can't afford to not use this service at any party. Don't rely on your "personality," to get you through your next event. Let's be honest, you're not much of a party person. I'm surprised people would even show up to a gathering you put together. For all I know, maybe they don't. But if you use my services, they will start!

There ain't no party like an Alfonso party. I am the world's best party villain and I want to make you the party hero!

Call 1-800-123-4567 to discuss rates and packages (not those kind of packages, ladies. I'm not talking about my penis. I'm talking about being compensated for services. Not those kind of services! Get your minds out of the gutter). Hire a professional party pooper today!

Chapter 4
DIRTY HAIKUS

Kids today don't know
The struggle of scrambled porn
Fuzzy nipple blur

Making love is hard
When your buttholes smell like poo
Life's an illusion

Idea for kid's show
Slap an orphan in his face
Tell him there's no god

Jesus was a man
Jesus was the son of god
Unless you're Jewish

Did you say something?
Wasn't paying attention
Looking at your tits

Let's play a game now
Close your eyes, and don't you peek
You were adopted

Giving this some thought
I don't like that Hitler guy
What was his problem?

Sometimes life is good
Sometimes life is really great
But your son is dead

Loose change, loose change, hmmm
Should I buy some gum? I just
Ejaculated

This soup tastes shitty
That's cause I shit in that bowl
You thought that was soup?

I got you popcorn
Go ahead, put your hand in
You like the surprise?

Poo on my face, now
Ew you are so god damn gross
I was just kidding

This soup tastes like dick
I made it with my smegma
Oh man, that's my fave!

Your breath smells like shit
I have some advice for you
Stop eating asshole

Roses are red and
Violets, they are blue so please
Just go fuck yourself

Oh, haven't you heard?
You are insignificant
Eat a bag of shit

Sex is wonderful
No, sex is totally gross
Whose fluid is this?

Life imitates art
Or does art imitate life?
I huff too much paint

ANTHONY KAPFER

I am an artist
That sounds better than saying
I live with my mom

I am an actor
That is how I justify
Being a waiter

I fucking hate you
You are always complaining
Third grade's not that hard

My father is dead
He is no longer alive
Also, pussy farts

My father is dead
He died doing what he loved
Abandoning me

Diarrhea fart
Oh my god I shit my pants!
Dreams really come true

Here is a haiku
A really dirty haiku
Fuck shit cock balls God

What if God is real?
And all atheists are wrong?
Ha. Yeah right. As if

Five syllables and
Then seven more syllables
And five more, then done

How do I love thee?
Eh, you're fine for now, I guess
Too lazy to cheat

Gargle gargle, gulp!
What the fuck?! Was that hot piss?
I asked for it cold!

Your mom likes anal...
izing repressed thoughts of strange
Fingers in her butt

Holy fucking shit!
Come to think of it, maybe
I let the dogs out

Take me drunk I'm home
My dreams killed my hopes and kids
I don't live to want

Life is but a dream
Death is but a nightmare, or
Other way around

Oh selfie stick man
You are what's wrong with the world
May your dick shrivel

Eating mounds of shit
Might sound like punishment, but
Some people like it

What to wear today?
Prosthetic boner, of course
Bleached my pubic hair

My favorite dance?
Scoliosis feather step
Life is meaningless

Pizza guy is here
Better put on some trousers
Oh, and a ball gag

The universe is
Infinitely expanding
Ha, that's what she said

Ironed my hamster
Swept up Grandma's old toe nails
I'm ready for bed

Boogers are funny
Fear the Illuminati
You are but a pawn

Continue to let
The New World Order rise up
You're doing so well

I really hate when
Alternate universes
Smell like dirty butts

You are a sucker
You paid money for this book
Ha, ha, ha, ha, ha

Got an erection
Was I at a funeral?
Oh yeah, probably

It's so bizarre how
All my fantasies involve
Gimp masks and relish

Take my word for it
Lube is no substitute for
Nondairy creamer

Stop it, that tickles
No whispering in my butt
Scream at my penis

My friend's mother died
What emoji should I use
In the, "Sorry," text?

Chapter 5
THE BJÖRK CHAPTER

This chapter of the book is dedicated to Björk, the greatest musical genius of our, or any time.

I don't know her personally, and if she ever read this book she would probably think, "This guy is pretty weird," which of course she would mean to be taken as a compliment, because Björk loves being weird. And I love Björk for being weird. And weird Björks me for being love. And love weirds Björk for being me. Wait what?

These jokes only make sense if you have a basic understanding of Björk and her music. If you do not, you might want to skip this chapter entirely. Don't worry; I won't be offended if you skip it.

Use the time you save to call a family member or a friend and tell them you love them. Or use the time to make a sandwich, or to empty your bowels.

Or make a sandwich and eat it while sitting on the toilet and emptying your bowels. The choice is yours. It's your extra time. Use it how you wish.

Question: Do you know the best thing about Björk?
Answer: Everything.

Björk doesn't fall in love. Love falls in Björk.

God worships Björk on the Sabbath.

Björk not only KNOWS music theory, she CREATED it.

You don't just listen to Björk. You have a religious experience.

Björk beat up Chuck Norris. Her voice knows karate.

Using the letters in Björk's full name, you can spell "Björk Is Gód." Then you have a bunch of leftover letters (like these: uðmunddttir)

When Björk says "Possibly Maybe," it means whatever she wants it to mean.

In six days Björk created the heavens, the earth, the sea and all that is in them. And on the seventh day she didn't even need to rest.

Björk's "Best Of" collection is her entire discography.

When I meet a woman, I rate her on a scale from one to ten Björks.

Question: Why did Björk cross the road?
Answer: Irrelevant. Björk doesn't need reasons for anything she does.

Question: What's the difference between Björk and God?
Answer: Björk is real.

Björk doesn't make mistakes. She makes innovations.

Question: If Björk sings in the woods, and no one is around to hear it, is it still awesome?
Answer: Yes.

Björk walks into a bar. The bartender says, "You are the most innovative musical artist who has ever lived."
The end.

Chapter 6
DRAWINGS

Wow, writing a book is hard. There are so many words! Maybe I can put a few drawings in this chapter, while I think of some more words to write in the next chapter. Wish me luck!

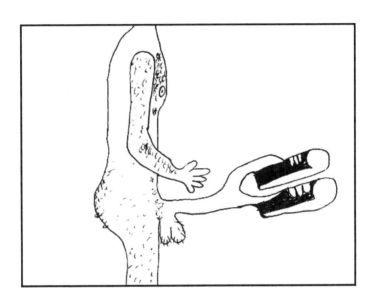

"See? I told you I had a two-foot penis!"

"I've been eating healthy lately, Doc. Today I ate grapes. Okay, okay, I drank a bottle of wine, but now you're really splitting hairs!"

The neighborhood got really dangerous when that unicycle gang rolled into town.

He laughed all the way to the sperm bank.

TALKING RECTANGLE

"So what brings you in here today?"
"Well, it's kind of oblong story."

BAD MAGICIAN

"For my first trick, I will make this rabbit disappear.
I'll need a fork, a knife, some salt, and pepper."

BAD MAGICIAN

"For my next trick, I'll make the rabbit reappear! I'll need a toilet, two ply toilet paper, and some privacy."

GUY WHO DOESN'T KNOW HOW TO TEXT EMOTICONS

LAZY FORTUNE COOKIE

Martian Humor

THE UNSURE PHILOSOPHER

"I think, therefore I am…I think…"

A receding hairline is your body's way of letting you know that you need to figure out what kind of hats you'll be wearing later in life.

"So, do you live with roommates?"
"No. I live with regret and disappointment, mostly."

"Son, you're 21 years old today. That means today is
the seven thousand six hundred and seventieth day of
the rest of your life."

"More like BOO-kakke!"

"Sorry I'm late. I couldn't find a spot. Parking is a nightmare, on Elm Street."

"Hey! Did you get a haircut?"
"No. It's just falling out."

"Dad, it's gotten to the point where we don't even talk anymore."

FINE ART

Ink on Sticky Note
By Anthony Kapfer
2016

Chapter 7
LOVE AT FIRST SIGHT

If you know me, and my past work, you already know I wrote and recorded a fake children's album, called Songs For Children To Cry To. Naturally, when I started working on this book, I decided I would write a fake children's story too! And here it is! (on the next page)

LOVE AT FIRST SIGHT

There is none greater in the world, than true love
True love is true, and it fits like a glove
It's honest and deep, perhaps sent from above
True love is more pure than the whitest white dove

I knew it when I first laid eyes on she
I, in a coffee shop, ordering tea
She, the barista, so full of glee
Her nametag said, "Hello, my name is Bree."

"What would you like?" She asked, looking ahead
  "Your hand in marriage, with you I thee wed
  But if you decline, which I must say, I dread
  I'll have a green tea, in a small cup, instead."

Bree looked displeased, and gave me a sneer
I stepped aside, trying to disappear
"It was not meant to be," I said inside my head
My proposal's denied and she wishes me dead

I sat, with my tea, and then what did I see?
The most beautiful woman I had seen, since Bree
She was drinking her coffee as black as the night
Black as my heart felt, since Bree and I's fight

I wonder if her name was pretty as she
I wonder if her name might somehow be Bree
For I already had a tattoo on my chest
It said, "Bree 4 Eva," but now I'm bereft

So if her name too, were perhaps Bree
That would be most convenient for me
I sat down beside her, and to my dismay
She looked unhappy, as if trying to say

"Hey! Okay! I must convey
That you cannot stay with me in this cafe
Nay! I say, I won't betray!
I have a fiancé and he's on his way!"

Then in walked a man, with a funny toupee
Mr. fiancé, his name was Ray
I knew that my welcome had been overstayed
He asked me to leave, or hell I would pay

With no delay, he gave me a punch
And I spilled all my tea on his lady's lunch
I quickly obeyed and I stood and I said
"I'll be on my way, and good day," to
the bunch.

So I left with a slink and I cried 'cause I knew
It was not meant be with girl number two
No one, not me, not a god could foresee
That I was about to meet girl number three

I opened the door to make a quick leave
And an angel appeared. I felt so relieved
I held the door open for her to walk in
And then I proposed, "Oh where have you been?"

"All of my life I've waited for thee
I finally found you. Please marry me."
Without even stopping, she said, "I must concede,
whether you beg, or whether you plead."

Then my heart sunk as I looked at her go
I couldn't believe my success was so low
She was the latest, the third in a row
But when feelings of woe come, I go with the flow

I walked to the bus stop and when it was there
I stepped up the steps, but I hadn't the fare
I had only one half of the regular price
The driver was pretty and witty and nice

She said, "You can step in honey, that will suffice."
I thanked her and said, "Now I'll be precise,
I want you to know that I've known from the start
That you drive the bus, the one in my heart."

She gave me a look and then yelled, "Take a seat!"
I did as she asked, and admitted defeat
The ride, it was long, and I felt incomplete
I was beat, I repeat, so I made my retreat

When I got home, I felt quite depressed
So I thought and I thought, while I took a long rest
I thought it best to sit back and assess
Where I went wrong, it was anyone's guess

Obsessed and distressed I'd become on my quest
And my poor little heart, it was put to the test
So lest I attest to invest in such zest
I turned to a pest when my love I professed

And so I digress, nonetheless from the stress
They say love is the best, so I feel no regrets
I am blessed for this mess. I am blessed to excess
I already can't wait to see whom I'll meet next

My question to you, do you think that it's strange?
Finding true love in this day and age?
I seem to find love fifty times in a day
I'm a romantic, what can I say?

Chapter 8
ACTING TIPS

Hi. My name is Actor Actorson, and I'm here to teach you everything you need to know about the art of acting. If you buy my book, "Act Like An Actor," you will learn literally millions of tricks of the trade, from an experienced professional.

I began my acting career as a young boy. My mother came into my room and asked, "What are you doing?" I said, "I'm doing my homework, mom." And she said, "Oh good. Keep up the good work." But I wasn't doing my homework. Inside of my textbook, was a comic book. I was just acting like I was doing homework. She totally believed me! It was at that moment I knew that I had found my true calling in life. From that day forward, I was an actor.

Here's an acting tip: Be yourself, unless the character you're playing is nothing like you. In cases such as this, it's best to be somebody else.

Did you know that acting is 80% standing around drinking coffee, while you wait for the crew to set stuff up, 15% holding in your pee, and 5% ACTING like you don't have to pee? You drank a lot of coffee, of course you have to pee! But if you buy my book, you'll be able to convince the world that you just used the facilities.

Acting tip numero two: Always use your eyebrows to express what you're feeling. Squint a lot. It will make it look like your character is thinking. "What's he/she thinking?" People will wonder. Everyone will think you are deep, even if you are shallow and stupid!

Acting is all about feeling comfortable on set. Sometimes the first day is a little stressful and awkward. But usually by the second day, I am feeling much more comfortable, which means, I take twice as much food from the craft services table. Sure, people stare, but I assume it's because they are taking mental notes of how they can be more like me.

I can teach you how to be a method actor. It's pretty simple, really. All you have to do is stay in character. Only answer to your character name, even in between takes.
If your character is rude, be rude to the cast and crew. Don't hold back. People will respect you for it. "What an artist," they will say to themselves, and each other. I have spent years perfecting the art of method acting.

Just the other day, I was on set, hanging out near the craft services table. My character was feeling pretty hungry, and I saw some granola bars just sitting there. My character loves granola bars, so being the method actor I am, I tried to see how many of those delicious treats I could fit into my pockets, while nobody was looking. I got them all! Luckily, I also love granola bars, so when I got home after a long day of acting, I was able to enjoy a tasty snack!

A good way to test your method acting techniques is to go on dates with people, and act like a different person. Come up with a character name and a backstory. But commit to it. Never break character. Try and see how weird you can get, while still being believable.

One of my favorite characters I've created in situations like this is named Dr. Brutus Von Coolfellow. He's been divorced twice; he likes to cut himself when he masturbates, because even though it hurts a lot, at least I know I can still feel something! It's a great acting exercise to shout that at the top of my lungs right in the middle of dinner, in a crowded restaurant. That really shakes things up.

Acting tip to the third power: If you stutter during your first take, stutter in the same place during every take after that, so the director and the other actors will think you made a conscious choice for that scene. They won't think you're an incapable, amateur loser. They will think you are a genius. I guarantee other actors will follow your lead and start stuttering up a storm. Now you're a trailblazer!

Even when you don't have a speaking role in a film, you can still do quite a bit of acting. You can convey a lot of emotions just but giving a look, or pointing to something, or falling down, or crying, or slapping a fellow actor. Just improvise, and never tell the other actors what you are going to do.

I like to think of acting like jazz. In jazz they say it's all about the notes you don't play. In acting, it's about the lines you don't say. Sometimes I don't say anything, even when I'm supposed to. It keeps the other actors on their toes. Silence can be so powerful.

Some of you might say, "Hey Actor, what makes you think you can write a book about acting? Haven't you exclusively been an extra? Isn't that not really the same as being an actor? Aren't you a disgrace to the art form, and to your family?" To which I would reply, "We, in the business, find the term 'Extra,' to be offensive. Technically, the term is 'Background ACTOR,' thank you very much. It even has actor right in the name. Plus, I give back stories to all my characters, and every single one of them has been an aspiring actor, so don't tell me I'm not an actor, buddy!"

Some of you might say, "You've mostly been in the background of home video footage at family gatherings, shot by various aunts and uncles. How does that make you an actor?" And I would tell you, "Look, just because these films haven't been widely released through some big time Hollywood studio, does not mean my work is not important. Please don't diminish my art because these films are low budget and filmed by members of my family, and not released in theaters." I'm so tired of people who can't appreciate a good indie film.

Just last week, I shot a film called, "Grandpa's 87th Birthday." It was really challenging, because my character doesn't feel comfortable around old people. I never know what to talk about. Plus, I find them to be gross. So I spent a lot of time acting like everything was fine, even though I couldn't wait until we were done shooting, and I could go home.

I did have a speaking role in this particular film. I said, "Grandpa, did you just fart, or does your living room always smell like this?" Everyone laughed, except for Grandpa. He actually looked pretty mad, but it could have just been the fact that he had such bad gas. I'm not really sure.

I thought the film was going to be a comedy, but later on there was an unexpected twist. Things took a dark turn, when Grandpa started choking on a granola bar he found on the floor. I thought I had grabbed them all, but I guess one of them had fallen out of my pocket. Anyway, Grandpa lost consciousness and hit his head on the coffee table. There was blood everywhere, and he had to be taken to the hospital. So I guess the film is more of a dark comedy/drama. It's so cool when films break the rules and cross genres!

I just got cast in the sequel to "Grandpa's 87th Birthday," which is tentatively titled, "Visiting Grandpa in the Hospital." Normally I don't do sequels, but because I loved the surprise ending of the first one, I made an exception. If I play my cards right, this could turn into a trilogy. I'm sort of thinking it'll be something along the lines of, "Grandpa's Funeral." He doesn't seem to be doing very well, but based on the first film, anything can happen, so who knows!

If you're like me and you've been bit by the acting bug, don't spray yourself with bug repellant, and don't rub any creams or balms on the bite. Let it fester. Buy my book, "Act Like an Actor," and start acting like a goddamn actor!

Chapter 9
DEEP CUTS

Some jokes are funny out loud. Some are funnier when you read them. This next chapter is full of little ideas and jokes that either never worked on stage or that I never tried on stage because I didn't think they would work. Call these the deep cuts, b-sides, scraps, leftovers, scraping the bottom of the barrel...

(look on the next page)

"Gah fex dlerp pid slomf"
Is how you say, "I'll have another shrimp cocktail,
please." in French, if you have a really weird accent.

I want to put together a female folk rock band that
funds all projects through crowdsourcing. They will be
called the Indiegogo Girls

I'm an adult with a smart phone. So I can text a friend
a photo of a woman peeing on a man, then immediately
check my recent bank transactions

These colors don't run. That's why America has such a
problem with type two diabetes.

They really got lazy when they named buildings.
"What are you building over there?"
"Oh this? It's a...ummm...it's a building."

Growing up in New York City has ruined certain
things for me. I can't enjoy eating almonds, because they
look like cockroaches with no legs.

"Et tutti, fruitti?" - Little Caesar

One time I broke up with a woman because I couldn't
hold in the fart anymore.

Autocorrect makes me so ducking mad

If used properly, a food dehydrator can become a thyme machine.

"Write!"
"What?"
"You know..."

Disguise the limit.

People hate Mondays. Wednesday is hump day. Thursday is the new Friday, which everyone thanks god for. Nobody gives a shit about Tuesday.

Guy: "Hey Arnold, what did you use to make your website? Was it Tumblr?"
Arnold Schwarzenegger: "It's not a Tumbla!"

I've got an itch. No, scratch that. Oh yeah, that's better.

Just once I wish a woman would treat me like a piece of meat, instead of like a side of vegetables.

Tragedy plus time machines equal comedy

Irish coffee is coffee with whiskey in it. Italian coffee is coffee with a slice of pizza in it.

People with glass kidneys shouldn't pass stones.

Sex cells

In the afterlife, you have to weigh the Necronomipros and the Necronomicons.

When someone takes a ton of photos of themself, and immediately looks at them and deletes the bad ones, they're being selfie destructive.

When you look uncomfortable in a selfie, it's called a "self conscious-ie."

I want to make sequels to all the 80's and 90's high school slacker movies about the main characters working as janitors at the same school.

Here is a really great pickup line women can use on men at bars that will work every time. "Hi."

I know I'm getting older because I saw a really attractive women littering, and it made me lose interest in her.

"I'm an actress."
-Some waitress

Customer to Waitress: "Have you ever acted in anything I might have seen?"
Waitress: "I was a waitress in a commercial for this restaurant."

According to my data, 100% of all statistics are statistics.

Do you want to know how an independent party can get at least 5% of the votes in the next election? Make the candidate legally change their name to Mickey Mouse.

My life's goal is to be really great at making vision boards. So I made a vision board with pictures of other vision boards on it.

From now on, I'm calling it Dunking Doughnuts.

Since all unicorns have horns, does that make their horns uniforms?

Brilliant idea: The One Cent Bill.

It's weird that the word "Umlaut," doesn't have an Umlaut in it.

Life: (SPOILER ALERT!) You die at the end.

Woman: "I'm not a crazy cat lady."
Translation: "I'm a crazy cat lady."

The last place I ever want to be is buried in a cemetery.

Recently I went through a really dark period. It was last night.

The act or instance of placing two or more things side by side? I'm juxtaposed to it.

"A good band Kansas is. Dust in the wind is all we are."
-Yoda

"Use divorce, Luke!"
- Obi-Wan Kenobi to Luke Skywalker after a few years of marriage

I aspire to be more sassy. I call this my sasspiration.

People who wear jeans and flip-flops look like they got almost all the way dressed, and then decided, "Eh, that's good enough."

Using a pay phone in New York City is the least fun way to get a disease.

Möbius Strip Poker: Playing strip poker on a continuous one-sided two-dimensional surface that can only exist in a three-dimensional space.

Möbius Trip: Falling down a staircase that has one fixed end and an opposite end that's twisted and joined to the fixed end. You fall forever.

I like my coffee like I like my punch lines: Preceded by an overdone premise.

You should never buy cheap toilet paper. You pay for it in the end.

If you do nice things for other people, you should receive a PhilanTrophy.

People in secret societies don't wear shoelaces because they get Illumin-knotty.

Some people say relationships are a two way street. I think they are more like five way intersections with no traffic lights.

Dating is weird. You spend a lot of time getting to know someone, then you break up and you spend the rest of your life trying to forget they ever existed.

If Jesus lived in modern times, he would totally use Super Soakers to baptize sinners

Be careful not to send texts with typos in them. You might give someone the wrong massage

Sometimes you have to get off your high horse, and get on your slightly lower horse. You're still better than people who don't have a horse

"This is the best thing since sliced Fred!" - A Cannibal

I have a collection of books that are so rare, they haven't even been written yet.

I've been reading this really long eBook for years. It's called the Internet. I have no idea how it ends. I'm trying to find out. Are there cliff notes? Is there a movie?

Chapter 10
THE DEPRESSED FOOD CRITIC

Los Enchiladas
By Stephen Lastname

I love this place more than I love some of my oldest friends. I say this, because I don't actually have any friends. If you're looking for authentic Mexican food, look no further. This is the place to go!

I regret many things in life, but none of them involve eating here. I have more fond memories of the pork tacos and the cactus tacos than I do about any of my ex-girlfriends. These tacos never once forced me to go shopping on a Saturday, for bookshelves and end tables, that I didn't want, by the way, only to take those same bookshelves and end tables with her when she left me a few months later. What I'm saying is, you should eat at this place. I do!

It is my favorite Mexican food in the universe...I think. I've only had Mexican food in this solar system, but I assume there is none better, anywhere.

Most of the time I am in there alone, but the staff is so friendly, it almost feels like I'm there with my friends. Actually, the staff is better than my friends because none of them can make food this great. Also they aren't real. I'm so alone in the universe, but when I eat here, I suddenly don't care!

This is the best Mexican food I have ever had. The chicken burritos are so good, that for a moment you will forget about your own mortality. That's quite a feat for me, because I think about the eventuality of death constantly. It's crippling a lot of the time.

The pork burrito will make you forget how insignificant we all are in this universe. The steak burrito will take your mind off of the fact that life is totally meaningless. Yum yum!

The fish tacos are so tasty; I almost forgot that my ex told me that I am the most miserable person she's ever met. When I think back about our relationship, I actually wish that instead of my ex, I spent my time with a 120-pound chicken taco from this place. That would have been way more fun! The sex would probably have been better too.
I once ate at Los Enchiladas on a first date, and for those few moments it didn't matter that one day both of us will be dead and gone. Forgotten for all of eternity. They make their own in house tortilla chips and the salsa is quite tasty!

I only hope my ex-girlfriend never finds out about this place, because she doesn't deserve an experience as pleasant and enjoyable as the one I had here. She is a rotten, no good, two timing monster who I hope lives a lonely, unfulfilling, miserable life that is void of the kind of human connection we all yearn for. This is a great place to go to on a date, or just with good friends!

Their rice and beans have accomplished more by being a delicious dish than I have in my entire life being an adult human being. It's flavorful and cooked to perfection. Mmm mmm. I, on the other hand, am none of those things. Sometimes I feel like I don't deserve love.

If you're looking for something fun to share with a few friends, try the nachos. I haven't had them because, as I said, I don't have anyone to share them with. Alright, fine, I lied. I ate an entire order while mumbling to myself, "You are a real pig aren't you? Who could ever love you? You don't deserve to taste these magnificent nachos!" No one seemed to notice or care, even though it was a clear cry for help.

When I find a place I like to go to, I am loyal and I stick with it. Looking back, that's probably one of the reasons my ex-girlfriend left me. She must have gotten tired of the same old routine. I think about that sometimes as I eat the chipotle chicken burrito alone and wonder where I went wrong in life.

The buffalo chicken quesadillas are another fine choice when dining there. Before I tasted them, I thought I would never feel love. I was totally numb, and I had no will to live, but these quesadillas made me feel human emotions again! Unfortunately, once I digested the food, I felt nothing once more. So I keep coming back!

I love this place, and so will you! I look forward to making some friends so that someday I can share this dining experience with another human!

Chapter 11
DATING PROFILES

Online dating is weird. If you've never tried it, read on, and experience it second hand, through this made up online dating scenario.

Username: DudeBro_420

About Me

I'm a real go-getter. I'm a laid back, chill person. I work hard, but I play harder. I use clichés to describe myself and that should be ok with you, because if you can't handle me at my worst, then you don't deserve me at my best.

What I'm Good At

Living life to the fullest, 24/7 365 (366 on every leap year! No rest for the wicked. I'll sleep when I'm dead).

What I'm Doing

What am I NOT doing? That's more like it, am I right? I'll tell you one thing I'm not doing. I'm not enjoying the love of another human being. It's been longer than I care to remember since somebody looked in my direction, let alone touched me. Sometimes I pretend to faint in a public place, just to feel the touch of a random Good Samaritan who rushes over to help me regain consciousness.

On Friday Night I Am

Either staying in, or going out. Dancing the night away, or calling it an early night and going to bed by 8pm. Donating my time at a soup kitchen, or getting into street fights with runaway teens. Doing blow off of a stripper's tits, or meditating. Enjoying the company of a friend, or curled up in the fetal position, thinking about all of my biggest regrets.

I Spend A Lot Of Time Thinking About

Things, stuff. Whether I'm working hard or hardly working. How much wood would a woodchuck chuck if a woodchuck could chuck wood. Peas and carrots, carrots and peas. How now brown cow. She sells sea shells by the sea shore. The rain in Spain stays mainly on the plains.

My hobbies. I have many. I collect things. I have a pretty extensive collection of hair and fingernails of all of my past lovers. I've even managed to snag some samples from people who didn't even know I exist. That was tough, but I take such pride in my collection. Dead cells are my life.

Six Things I Can't Live Without

1. Oxygen (hee hee)
2. Water (I'm so clever)
3. Food (are you in love yet?)
4. Sleep
5. Friends
6. Sex ;-)

You Should Contact Me If

You want to. You're not afraid to get real with someone. You're okay with the fact that I live in what used to be my parent's attic. Now it's my bachelor pad. A lot of my old childhood toys are up here, so there's always plenty of cool stuff to play with here. I do sleep in my old childhood crib. But don't worry. The bars have been removed. I wear big boy pants now! I hardly ever fall out of bed anymore. My mom lives downstairs, which is great. If you're lucky you'll get to meet her.

Also, ideally you would be a cat person. I have a small army of cats in my apartment. Last time I counted it was in the ballpark of 36 or so. Most of them have names, but I'm starting to lose track of them all. It's a lot of hard work taking care of those little guys and gals, but it gives my life a sense of worth. Although it's gotten to the point where I don't go outside much anymore. If you love cats, maybe our first date could be here at my place. I call it the Cat Cave. You get it? Like the Bat Cave, but with an unhealthy amount of cats. You could help me feed all of the cats (they each have very specific dietary restrictions, and some need special medical care. One cat is diabetic, one is vegan, one eats its own poop exclusively, and another eats my poop exclusively). I would also like to know right off the bat if my cats like you. It's very important that they do. They are very overprotective of me. The last person I dated wasn't a cat person, and was subsequently murdered by several of my cats. It was not a pretty sight, but I appreciated the honesty of these cats. Also I've eaten human flesh, so please be open-minded when it comes to alternative diets. I'll eat your little tofu dish, or whatever. I expect the same respect in return.

Username: SunLover69

About Me

I'm a laid back person, looking for someone to get weird with. I do have a son, so please be okay with that.

What I'm Good At

A gentleman never asks, and a lady never tells ;)

What I'm Doing

;)

On Friday Night I Am

Wouldn't you like to know

I Spend A Lot Of Time Thinking About

Will my son ever take out the garbage?

Six Things I Can't Live Without

My son

Hot sex

THAT'S ALL I NEED!

You Should Contact Me If

You think you can handle me

INBOX

DudeBro_420
Hi. U R cute ;)

SunLover69
Hey. Thank U. I also think you are a QT

DudeBro_420
How's your day goin'?

SunLover69
Good. You?

DudeBro_420
It would be better if you sent nudez ;)

SunLover69
You first

DudeBro_420
I asked first :-o

SunLover69
Nope!

DudeBro_420
Your so mean!

SunLover69
You're*

DudeBro_420
Go die!

SunLover69
You first

DudeBro_420
Make me

SunLover69
Today's youth is doomed

DudeBro_420
Agreed! I love you!

SunLover69
I love you more

DudeBro_420
Let's get married

SunLover69

Ok, but first, what's your favorite activity?

DudeBro_420

I love a good existential crisis

SunLover69

Me too! I'm having one now

DudeBro_420

Really? About what?

SunLover69

I was thinking, "What if all of this is already all planned out, and I'm powerless to decide what happens next?"

DudeBro_420

If you're powerless, you should send me nudez! Lolz

SunLover69

What if none of this is even real? What if we are just imaginary beings created in a computer somewhere? We could be nothing more than computer code being written in binary by some nerd with too much time on their hands

DudeBro_420

01110011 01100101 01101110 01100100 00100000
01101101 01100101 00100000 01101110 01110101
01100100 01100101 01111010

SunLover69
What's that?

DudeBro_420
It means, "Send me nudez," in binary

SunLover69
Bye!

DudeBro_420
00
1

SunLover69
What?

DudeBro_420
That's supposed to be two boobs and a penis

SunLover69
Martin, this is your mother. I made a fake account
because it's the only way I could think of to get your
attention. Will you take out the trash? You are 21 years
old. I shouldn't have to tell you to do these things! You
are lazy and unappreciative of all the work I do around
here.

DudeBro_420
MOM???!!!

SunLover69
Yes?

DudeBro_420
Send nudez. LMFAO!

SunLover69
I wish you're father had pulled out

DudeBro_420
Your*

Chapter 12
THE MASS EMAIL

Hey Friends!

Please excuse this mass email. I'm writing to all of you at once to save some time. As you all know, I've been extremely busy lately. Who has time to write individual personal emails anymore, you know?

How are you doing? I hope you're doing okay. Especially after everything that's happened.

I'm really sorry to hear that you lost your job/your father died/you're getting divorced/you have to go to rehab.

Phil, losing your job must be a real bummer. I can't even imagine what you are going through right now. Mostly because I have lots of money saved, so if I lost my job, I'd be ok for quite a while, but I heard you have no savings at all. Sorry bro.

Charles, your dad was a great man. This must be an extremely hard time for you. Just know that your father died doing what he loved, having a heart attack. It's funny you mention death though. I was just teaching my little nephew, Spencer about it. I told him one day we are all going to be dead, and he said the cutest thing. He said, "But for how long?" I hear the wake is on Wednesday. Spencer and I will see you there! I can't imagine what it must be like, because my dad is alive and well. In fact, I just had lunch with him the other day. I love him so much. He says hello, by the way.

Ashley, getting divorced must really be hard on everyone involved. I heard your husband changed the locks one day and skipped town with the kids. I also heard that you were forced to move back in with your mother. I ran into your mom a few weeks back, before your life fell apart, and we had a really nice conversation about humming birds. She's a great lady. Tell Gail I finally decided that my favorite bird is the flamingo. Anyway, I'm sure you'll be glad to know that my wife and I are doing great. Also my parents are still happily married, so I really can't relate to what you're going through on any level, but still, I'm sorry.

Patrick, we all knew you'd end up in rehab eventually. Maybe it will be fun. It could be a good chance to meet some new people you have things in common with. I was thinking about it earlier, and I started wondering, do you think anyone has ever ruined their life because of non-alcoholic beer? That would be so funny! Would they have an opposite intervention? They show up someplace where they aren't invited and ask for help. Their whole family would be like, "Look, you're really boring and no one wants you here. Maybe if you started drinking you'd be more fun to be around." But in all seriousness, you have a real problem. Your family is really taking this whole thing pretty hard.

I realize that you guys don't all know each other, so I've CC'd everyone in this email. I thought it would be helpful if you had each other's contact information so you can introduce yourselves. Maybe you'll become friends and cheer each other up.

Phil, before you got laid off, you were a lawyer. Maybe you can be Ashley's divorce lawyer. Also, you've been single for a while, right? Maybe after Ashley's divorce is finalized, you two might hit it off, and then who knows! I think I hear wedding bells already!

Charles, you should talk to Patrick about how your father never told you he loved you before he died. That might make Pat feel better about his own life, and maybe he will stop drinking so much.

Anyway, sorry again. I gotta run now. I'm having drinks with my boss, my dad, and my wife. Talk to you all soon! Hang in there.

Sincerely yours,
-Doug

Chapter 13
CAR CRASH

I thought for this part of the book, I would write about a real thing that happened to me. This part of the book will be less silly, but I will try and keep it fun.

When I was 27 years old, I almost died. That's right, I almost joined the 27 club. Kurt Cobain, Jimi Hendrix, Janis Joplin all died at 27. Luckily, I didn't die. I think it was mostly because I wasn't famous enough to be a part of the 27 club. Here is what happened:

On May 21, 2012 I did a comedy show at Bowery Poetry Club, in NYC. After the show, I was driving home in the rain. It was about 3:30 in the morning.

I hit a slippery patch on the highway and hydroplaned. I lost control of the car, which spun and hit a wall. I hit my head. I don't remember the impact or the next 15 or 20 minutes after that. What I do know, is that there were no other cars involved in the accident, which I am very thankful for.

My next memory is fifteen minutes later, mid conversation with a cop. I was standing outside of my car, explaining to him what happened. He said an ambulance was on the way. I said, "Oh that's okay, I don't need the ambulance, I'm alright." I had amnesia, a broken neck and a collapsed lung. My body was in shock. The cop must have thought I was a lunatic. The cop told me he got the call 15 minutes earlier. I didn't have any memories of the crash or the time in between. I was confused. I thought, "How could he have gotten the call 15 minutes ago? This just happened." I started to realize I had amnesia. I still don't know if I was fully conscious or not in those fifteen minutes that have been wiped from my memory.

The ambulance came and I stepped inside. I talked to the EMTs about what I remembered. I think I mostly babbled nonsense.

At the hospital they cut off all my clothes. My Minor Threat t-shirt and my good jeans were ruined. I remember saying, "Are you cutting my jeans? God Damn it!" Inside the pocket of my jeans was the money I got paid for the show I did earlier that night. I never saw that money again.

They put me in a temporary room for a few hours. I was naked, except for a sheet that covered me. They did some X-rays and some other tests to check my injuries. The doctors were nervous that my brain was bleeding. A brain surgeon came in to talk to me about what the surgery would entail if my brain was in fact bleeding and about the possibility of spinal surgery. I was lucky enough that none of those things were an issue. My neck was going to heal on its own. I fractured two vertebrae (numbers five and six).

Basically, pieces of the vertebrae chipped but stayed attached and in place. This meant it would heal all by itself. They slapped a neck brace on me. They said I had to wear it for six to eight weeks. They said my brain wasn't bleeding and I didn't need brain surgery.

There was one procedure that needed to be done. In the accident, the seatbelt collapsed my lung and I guess I had some kind of internal bleeding. They told me they needed to insert a tube into my chest cavity.

The tube would suction out the blood and air that was filling my chest cavity and keeping my lung collapsed. They numbed the incision area with Lidocaine. Then I got shot up with Morphine. I felt the muscles in my arms and legs relax.

The doctor made an incision on the side of my chest and started shoving the tube in me. I screamed like someone was killing me. I felt the tube making its way around my muscles. It took several minutes before they were done pushing it through. The Morphine never really kicked in.

I had my cell phone and was able to make some phone calls when I first arrived, which was around five in the morning. Some of my best friends came to see me around eight. They were freaked out and tearing up. I was cracking jokes. I was lucky to be alive, and the last thing I wanted to do was complain or be a bummer.

I told my friends to get some footage of me in the hospital. We were filming comedy shows and behind-the-scenes footage for a documentary and I realized that this hospital stay would be expensive. This was now a big budget movie. I wanted to take advantage.

Eight hours later, they moved me to my actual room. I had a window, and there was art on the wall. My roommate was very friendly. He was an older man with long hair. He was always sneaking outside to have a smoke. He told all of the doctors that I was a comedian. One of them took my information and actually watched some of my videos online. This guy was doing PR for me while I was lying in a hospital bed. He was great.

It was funny to watch him lie to the nurses about how much pain he was in. They came around with pain medication, and asked, "On a scale of one to ten, how much pain are you in?" Every time he would say, "I'll be honest doc, I'm at about a nine." Then they would turn and ask me, (the guy with the broken neck and the tube shoved up in between his ribs, wrapped around his muscles) and I would always say, "I don't know, I guess I'm at about a four out of ten."

I didn't want to get hooked on pain medication. It seems counterproductive to leave the hospital with a drug problem, in addition to everything else.

One day the doctor came to talk to me about my injuries. He told me that the seatbelt was the cause of the collapsed lung. It is also the reason I was alive. No one ever really tells you that seatbelts can hurt you while they save you. The doctor said, "A lot of tall lanky people are prone to this injury."

I was surprised by his choice of words. He could have called me tall and skinny. He could have said if I had more body fat or muscle mass, the seatbelt would not have injured me so badly, but he referred to me as tall and lanky. He was literally adding insult to injury. I appreciated that.

I asked the doctor about the hole they cut into my side, "How bad is the scar going to be?" He answered with a phrase I never thought I'd hear a doctor say. He said, "Don't worry, chicks will dig it."

I was in bed for days, not really sure how badly I was actually hurt. I didn't remember the accident, and I didn't get a good look at my car, so I had no idea what the damage was like. This didn't seem real. I kept telling the story to people, but since I didn't actually remember being there, it was hard to wrap my head around.

I had a plastic container that I had been peeing in, so I had not gotten out of bed yet. But by day two or three, I had to take a shit. This is something I had been doing on my own for many years. Suddenly it wasn't that simple. I was attached to a machine that was suctioning the blood and air out of my chest cavity, which would then allow my lung to re-expand. The machine was plugged into the wall. This meant in order for me to get up and go to the bathroom, a nurse needed to come and unhook the suction machine from the wall. Then they handed me the machine that was connected to my tube, which I had to carry with me into the bathroom. But they didn't have to come in with me. I did all of that by myself.

As I took my first steps in forty-eight hours, I realized how hurt I was. My head felt like it weighed a hundred pounds. I was sore everywhere. Using the bathroom was incredibly hard and frustrating. I had to place the suction machine down on the floor next to the toilet, in order to do my business. After I was done, the nurse had to come reconnect everything, turn the suction back on, and then help me back into bed. This all took about twenty minutes. I was physically and mentally exhausted. It was the most depressing shit I had ever taken.

I felt helpless and weak. But I was making progress.

Two days after an accident that could have killed me, I sat up, got out of bed, and walked around. I went to bed feeling mildly accomplished.

The next day started out poorly. I didn't sleep well. I was tired of lying in the same position all day every day. I was still attached to the machine, even though the doctors thought I would be off of it by this point. I was frustrated. I felt beaten.

A physical therapist came in to talk to me. He asked if I could walk. I told him my legs worked fine. He helped me out of bed and we walked around the halls together. It felt great. When we got back to my room, he brought me a chair to sit in. I sat in the chair all day. It made me feel like myself again. I wasn't bed ridden.

My friends came to visit. They were happy to see me out of bed. It was almost like we were just hanging out. Everyone was sitting around talking and laughing. I felt good.

The next day, I woke up in a lot of pain. The tube in me was really starting to hurt. I told the nurse. It took a long time for her to do anything about it.

Eventually a bunch of doctors came in to look at me. They crowded around my bed. They said maybe the tube moved out of place. They took off the bandages that were covering the big ugly hole where the tube was shoved inside me. Then they started shoving it back into place. I screamed in agony. It hurt worse than the first time they jammed that thing in my side. My insides were already sore from the tube being in there for so long.

Also I wasn't on any pain medication this time. After a few minutes of this, they redressed the wound and left me. I was nearly in tears. Fifteen or so minutes later the nurse came in and gave me oxycodone and Toradol. Then she left. I couldn't move. Fifteen or twenty minutes later those medications kicked in. I didn't feel anything. It was amazing. I had earned this. I don't remember much of the rest of that day.

While I was in the hospital, all of my comedy friends were coming by to see me. We talked about a show that was coming up. We were all supposed to perform. Obviously I wasn't going to make it.

They decided they would keep my slot, and they were all going to do my act. Everyone went up and did a few of my jokes each. Then they all got together and sang one of my songs together, like a choir. They showed me the footage. It was amazing. I was in the hospital, but my jokes were still out there in the world.

A couple of days later, I had another show booked. I asked Ricky Wells to go do the show as me. He agreed.

No one there knew who I was, so they didn't even realize what was happening. It was our little secret joke. I was introduced, "Ladies and gentleman, Anthony Kapfer," and Ricky Wells got up and did my whole act. I also got to see this footage. All of this helped me get through those long, hard days at the hospital.

Days continued to pass. I was scared that my lung wasn't healing. I had an air leak, which meant there was a still a small hole. It also meant I still needed the tube and the machine.

Doctors came in and talked to me about the possibility of surgery. There were three different options they spoke about. I was never really sure which one was a possibility for me.

The first option was that a damaged part of my lung would be removed. Another option was that my lung would be stapled closed. The staples would eventually dissolve on their own. The last option was they would insert a camera inside me, and blow some kind of powder onto my lung and scar tissue would form, closing the hole. None of these options sounded good to me. I was scared.

After a full week in the hospital, they decided to take the tube out of me. I was worried about the amount of pain I would feel as the tube slid passed my muscles and ribs, luckily, the tube coming out was much quicker, and much less painful than when it went in. It felt great to not be connected to it. It was much easier to get out of bed by myself. Going to the bathroom was easier. I was in less pain, but I still couldn't go home. They were still monitoring my lung. There was still a hole and if it didn't close up, they would have to re-insert the tube and operate on me. That was scary.

Every morning at five o'clock, I would have X-rays done. Then I would sit around and wait for a doctor to come in and talk to me about how my lung was doing. They never came.

Apparently, no news is good news. If my lung was bad, they would have come in and talked to me, but since it was okay, they didn't have to tell me anything. I didn't really know this at the time, so I was really nervous and confused.

I had an attractive nurse. She was working the night shift on one of my last nights in the hospital. She kept coming into the room and talking to me. I told her about the accident. We also talked about other things. It wasn't like the way the other nurses talked to me.

She was young, maybe younger than me. She laughed at my jokes. I thought maybe she might be flirting with me. Then she asked me, "When was your last bowel movement." It was then that I knew she wasn't flirting with me. She went about her business, and I went to sleep.

After ten full days, I was finally well enough to go home. The hole in my lung had closed on it's own. I didn't need surgery. I got dressed, and they wheeled me downstairs in a wheelchair, because that's what they do. I thought about how lucky I was. I broke my neck, but I walked out of the door of that hospital.

I spent the next few days at home, resting, and working on new jokes. I watched a lot of movies. One of them was Annie Hall. There is a scene where Woody Allen's character asks Annie Hall if she had ever been to Coney Island. In the next scene, they are driving to Coney Island, on the same highway I was driving on when I had my accident. They pass the same exit I crashed near. That made me strangely happy. If you have to hit a wall in your car, let it be the Annie Hall wall.

Six days after getting out of the hospital, I made my return to stand-up comedy. It was at a bar in Brooklyn. I had tons of new jokes about neck braces and hospitals. A bunch of my friends came out to see me. And with a broken neck, I took the stage and made people laugh. I was back.

106

I spent the next few weeks performing comedy with my neck brace. Some people thought the neck brace was an act. They thought I was doing a character. That might have partially been my fault. I thought it would be funny to buy a t-shirt that said, "Women's Wrestling Champion of the World." I wore it almost every day. It's the same shirt Andy Kaufman used to wear. Andy Kaufman also wore a neck brace for a short time, but not everyone got the reference. Either way, lots of people on the street would look at me, with my neck all messed up, then look down and read my shirt, and laugh. Mission accomplished.

I wore that neck brace for most of the summer. I had to keep it on all the time. I showered in it. I slept in it. It was rough. The heat made it even more unpleasant. I was also tired of people on the street looking at me funny. I couldn't wait for the neck brace to come off. I was nervous that when it finally came off, I would have a tan line in the shape of a neck brace and people would continue to look at me strangely.

Eventually, my neck and lung healed and I kept doing comedy. I had to stop telling all of my neck brace jokes, though. I was sad to see them go, but happy to not be injured anymore.

So what's the moral of this story? I don't know? Wear your seatbelt? Maybe. Don't die in a car accident? Sure. Who knows? Just live and be happy, because things can always be worse.

Oh by the way, chicks totally dig the scar.

(There are some great photos on the next page!)

Photo by Ricky Wells

This is a photo of the damage to my car after the accident.

This photo was taken after I got out of the hospital. It was the first time I had seen how bad my car looked. I was still pretty sure I could drive it home, but the people at the towing company said I could not. So I let them send it to a junkyard.

That car and I had some good times together, except for that last part, where I crashed into a wall. Sorry car!

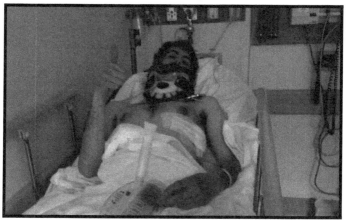

Photo by Ryan McCormick

This is the first picture taken of me in the hospital.

This was taken after they shoved that tube inside of my chest, but before I had my own hospital room.

I was naked under the sheet. They hadn't given me a hospital gown yet. They just slapped the neck brace on, and tossed me aside. I was there for about twelve hours before I got a real room.

I gave the thumbs up because I was not dead!

Photo by Erin Laure Jennings

This is a picture of me looking cool in my hospital room.

I'm not naked in this one. I was wearing a gown. I felt like the belle of the ball. With the shades on, you don't even notice the neck brace!

Photo by Anthony Kapfer

This is a picture from my point of view.

This was a wonderful continental breakfast that was served to me in my hospital room. Eggs, a pre-wrapped slice of bread, a muffin, cereal, milk, and orange juice. Yum!

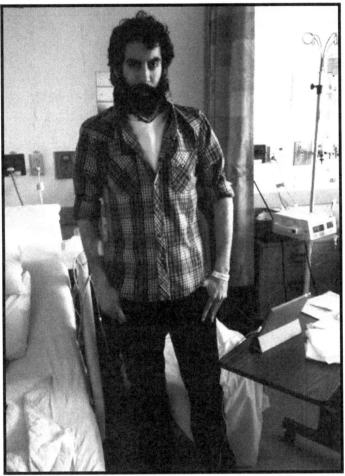

Photo by Stephanie Werner

This is a picture of me on the last day of my hospital stay.

I got to wear real clothes again, for the first time in ten days! The neck brace made a really fun and fashionable accessory.

Photo by Ricky Wells

This is a picture of me on stage during my first performance after my accident.

You can tell I'm having a great time playing guitar and telling jokes, while wearing my cool neck brace!

Photo by Erin Laure Jennings

This is another picture of me on stage. Look how much fun I'm having!

I tried really hard to stay positive during my time at the hospital. I tried to make jokes and goof off. I tweeted a lot. I figured if I was going to be in bed all day every day, I could try and turn it into a bit. Here are a bunch of my favorite tweets from the hospital. That's right, I am including tweets in this book. Deal with it.

HOSPITAL TWEETS
@AnthonyKapfer

May 22, 2012
I just drove in from a car accident, and boy is my lung punctured.

Just lying around watching Telemundo, on pain pills.

Going to the hospital is like going on vacation to the worst place ever.

I just had my first sponge bath. It's not as sexy as I had hoped.

May 23, 2012
I wonder if this hospital has continental breakfast.

What's the deal with being knocked unconscious after a car crash? That's no time for a nap!

You think anyone ever sent a dick pic from a hospital bed?

I got out of bed for the first time since the accident. My legs work.

May 24, 2012

You guys ever break your neck and puncture a lung at the same time? Eh, I don't recommend it. You're not missing much.

Best part about being in the hospital...bendy straws!

May 26, 2012

Gotta love salisbury steak night at the hospital.

I haven't worn pants in 5 days

May 29, 2012

Been getting a lot of positive feedback about my hospital tweets. Should I hurt myself again and stay here a few more days?

May 30, 2012

I had my chest tube taken out. I'm no longer half man, half machine. Now I'm just boring.

I'm such a rockstar. I had a comedy show last Monday, crashed a car, and I've been doing drugs for the past 8 days.

June 1, 2012

They just wheeled me downstairs. Waiting for a cab. I'm wearing real clothes again! This concludes the live tweeting of my hospital stay.

Wouldn't it be so funny if the cab I took home from the hospital got into a terrible accident, and I ended up right back here?

Chapter 14
BUFFER

Okay, okay. I'm sorry. I was going to end the book with that last chapter, but that was a little heavy, wasn't it? I can't end it that way.

I also didn't think it would make sense to jump right back into some silly short story, or essay, or dumb poem, so this section of the book is sort of just a buffer. Hopefully I can lighten the mood, and prepare you for the last few chapters of the book.

The question is, what do I put in this chapter? That is still unclear.

Do you need to use the restroom? I should have asked earlier, but if you are reading this book all in one sitting, this would be a good time to put it down and go. Although you could very easily continue reading while you sit on the toilet.

Some people might wonder what my process is when I'm writing. Some of you might be imagining me sitting at a desk, in front of a nice computer, or an old typewriter, typing away. That's how I imagine a lot of professional authors do it. As for me, I wrote most of this book on my phone, while sitting on a New York City train.

Right now in fact, I'm riding the subway on my way to perform stand-up comedy. I'm passing the time by writing this. I'm pretty sure it will actually make it into the book. You are totally reading this!

A man on this train just took some bongos out of a case and started tuning them. Then, another man with a guitar got on. He sat down next to the bongo dude. The bongo dude looked at the guitar guy and was like, "All we need now is a trumpet player." So far, there's no sign of any trumpet players. But I still have hope! You might call me a dreamer, but I do believe they will start their bongo, guitar, and trumpet trio!

If I was writing this book in a boring, stuffy old office, you would not have gotten to read that awesome bongo story. I'm really changing the game right now. The writing books game, that is.

Now, I'm writing this paragraph at home. Several hours have passed since that last paragraph. That's the magic of books. To you, only a few seconds have passed since you read my awesome bongo train story. Is your mind blown yet? Time is relative. Reality is an illusion.

I do hope my book isn't making you spiral into a paranoid nervous breakdown, but you should be aware that everything we think to be true is a lie told to us to keep us trapped in our own private prisons.
But I know you didn't buy this book to hear about all of that. You bought this book to read some funny things that I wrote. You paid to have me make you laugh. You paid

good money, too! And what am I doing? Stalling, that's what. What am I waiting for? Do I not have any more ideas about what to write in the next chapter?

If you skipped ahead to the next chapter to see if the rest of the pages are blank, you have either overestimated or underestimated my artistic integrity, and my capacity to write an entire book. I'm not sure which one it is yet, but I assure you, there will be more chapters for you to read. But we are going to get there at my pace. I am directing this journey, and you have to trust me. Without trust, we have nothing.

Maybe this would be a good opportunity to play a game. Not many books attempt to play games with the reader. Ready?

Okay think of a number between 1 and infinity. Was it 666? No? 69? No?!!! Shit. This game is too hard. Okay, forget that game.

Okay let's try a different game. I bet I can read your mind. Right now you're thinking, "This book is really weird. This guy is trying to read my mind. So far, every word he is predicting is precisely what I am hearing in my head! I've got to stop reading this book. Get out of my head, Anthony!" How did I do? I nailed it, didn't I?

Chapter 15
DATING A VEGAN

One time, I met a woman at a party. We really hit it off. We had a lot in common. For instance, she was a model, and I'm a really big fan of models. Things couldn't have been better, or so I thought.

There was one big problem though. She was a vegan, and she said she only dated guys who were also vegan. I know that, because she told me within thirty seconds of meeting her.

This tends to be my experience with many vegans. So I thought to myself, "Well I guess I'm a vegan now." The trouble was that I'm not actually a vegan, but when the truth won't get you what you want, you gotta make stuff up.

I was going to commit to this lie for as long as I had to. Not when I was alone or with friends, just when I was around her. If it came down to it, I would live out the rest of my life, clinging to my fake veganism.

I was willing to lead a double life, as a man who sneaks out in the middle of the night to a 24-hour diner, to order a sub-par steak. Every bite would feel like ecstasy and agony, simultaneously.

Sure, the sweet, sweet flesh would satisfy my every need, but the guilt afterwards would be excruciating. But what was I supposed to do, tell her the truth? That's preposterous.

So anyway, back at the party, we made plans to go on our first date. I let her pick the place because I'm a gentleman, and also I had no idea where to take her. What do vegans eat, anyway? Where do they hang out? I sure as heck don't know, even to this day.

I can't say the name of the place she wanted to go to, because they are a big corporation, but I can say it sounds like, "Hole Foods." She grabbed some food and we sat down at a table. She had the vegan sushi and I had nothing. I told her I was full.

Things were going pretty well, until she asked me a question that I was not prepared to answer. "What's your favorite vegan dish?" she asked, casually, but somewhat suspiciously.

I'll be honest, I did zero research before this date. So, I said the first thing that came to mind. "Uhhhh, I eat a lot of salads," I said, with as much confidence as I could muster.

I thought that was a good answer, but she wasn't satisfied. Maybe it was because I couldn't make eye contact when I said it. Maybe it was because I laughed as I said it. It just sounded so ridiculous.

What am I, some kind of yak, roaming around the pasture? I ain't no yak, I'll tell you that. I'm a red blooded

American man! So, naturally I giggled when I lied about eating salad.

I think she might have noticed. She gave me a look that suggested, "You're a god damn liar." She quickly fired back with a follow up question. "What do you like to put in your salads?"

Oh no! I thought I was in the clear with my original answer. But now I had to create a custom salad off the top of my head! I mentally went down the list of things I like to put in my salads. Chicken, cheese, bacon. No. None of these will do. I can't tell her any of this. She would be so angry. I was starting to panic! I could not think of a single acceptable thing to put in a salad.

And then it came to me. Portobello mushrooms. I love mushrooms, and I was excited to talk about it because I knew we were about to have our first genuine moment of bonding. We were going to talk about how much we loved Portobello mushrooms for the rest of the date. Afterwards, we would embrace lovingly. We'd start dating exclusively and come up with pet names for each other. Eventually, I would propose to her on a mushroom farm. Soon after, we would surely be married. I pictured her after the ceremony, throwing a big bouquet of portobello mushrooms to her bridesmaid friends. My mind skipped through the next few years, and the next few after that. I thought about our future daughter. Of course we would name her Bella. Life would be good.

But that's not the way it happened. Once I said the words, "Portobello mushrooms," she proclaimed, "Yuck! I hate mushrooms!" And she ruined everything.
It was at that moment I knew we weren't meant to be. It wasn't the fact that we had nothing in common, or the

fact that I was lying through my teeth the entire date. No. It was definitely this mushroom thing.

We sat for a moment in silence, for what felt like an eternity. I wished she'd say something, anything. Then finally she did. "What did you have for breakfast today?"

"God damn it! What is it with this woman and food?" I asked myself in my head. I longed for that unbearable silence from earlier. At least then I wasn't being interrogated. I racked my brain for more vegan foods I could blurt out casually, but I was drawing a blank. She was looking at me intently, waiting.

Knowing I needed to say something, I opened my mouth and started speaking, without knowing what was going to come out. "I…uhhh…had…a big ole bowl of leaves." What had I done? I quickly shut my mouth, for fear I would make things even worse. Would she buy this load of bologna? I sat and waited for her response.

She sat for a while, thinking. Finally, she said, "This isn't working. I know what you're doing, and I don't appreciate it. You're kind of a jerk. Eat shit."

And I yelled out to her, "I can't, I'm vegan."

Chapter 16
GYM MEMBERSHIP

There's a gym in my neighborhood. I walk by it every day on my way home. Usually, I pretend I'm jogging when I pass the window with all the people on treadmills, so they can be jealous that I am doing the real version of what they are doing, and mine doesn't cost any money.

One day I went inside to check out the place. Okay, fine, you caught me. I went inside to use the bathroom because my roommate ate some, "vintage clams," he bought on the Internet. Needless to say, the bathroom looked and smelled like a warzone. I was not about to deal with that. Who knew clams do not age well, as a fine wine does.

Anyway, I went inside the gym and somehow I ended up with a one-year membership, which would be funny, if you knew me. I'm not the kind of guy who works out. I'm in such bad shape; I get out of breath while eating.

The only lifting I do is when I lift a chicken leg to my mouth! The only curls I do are curly fries! The only diet I'm on is diet cola!

I don't know how it happened. The guy behind the counter was very aggressive. He wouldn't take no for an answer. I don't even remember a lot of it. He started telling me about the different membership packages they offer, then I sort of blacked out.

When I came to, I had a receipt for my one-year gym membership in one hand, and a free t-shirt with the gym logo on it, in my other hand.

They give the free t-shirts out so that you feel less like you were just robbed, and more like you just got an awesome deal. Nobody robs you AND gives you stuff, right? But make no mistake about it, t-shirt or no, I had just been hoodwinked.

I kept passing by the gym every day on my way home, but never went inside. The guy who signed me up sat at a desk by a giant window that overlooked the sidewalk. He could see me walking by every single time. At first we would wave at each other as I passed, mostly deciding to go to a bar and get drunk, instead of trying to get in shape.

Working out is hard, but when I'm drunk, I feel like I can do anything. If I have enough whiskey in my system, I feel like the strongest man in the world! So, I didn't really see the need for exercise. Is exercise going to help me forget all of my sorrows and mistakes? Is exercise going to rid me of my crippling self-doubt? Is exercise going to give me the confidence I need to get out of bed in the morning? I think not!

Day after day, I kept walking by the gym without ever stepping foot inside that place. I was less interested in exercising than I was before I had been tricked into joining this work out cult. The gym guy realized I had no intention of ever using my membership. That's when things got weird.

He started putting passive aggressive signs in the window that said things like, "Work out today, or you will forever be a worthless slob," and, "I know you know I see you. Keep walking. This place is for people who are serious about their health!" I think I may have hurt his feelings.

I eventually started avoiding eye contact with him. I'd pretend to get a call on my cell phone as I walked by, just so we didn't lock eyes. I couldn't take that look that said, "Come on man, don't you want to at least work out once before the year ends?" I was doing a great job avoiding this guy, but I could see with my peripheral vision that he was really bummed out. I swear, one day I thought I saw him crying.

Sometimes he would see me, and come outside to talk to me. He'd say stuff like, "Hey man, what's up? Where are you going?" For a while I'd make up excuses. I'd pretend I had stuff going on but I never had anything to do. I would say things like, "I've got to go. Tonight I'm cleaning out my snake tank." I don't have a snake! Not anymore, anyway. My pet rat ripped his head right off. It was pretty gruesome. But that is a story for another time.

Sometimes I'd say, "Sorry buddy, I wish I could come inside and do exercise things, but it's my second cousin's fifth anniversary of the time she ate so many gummy worms, she puked blood all over the wedding dress she was trying on, just for fun. They made her buy the dress, because it was ruined, on account of all the blood. Since then, every year, we pretend to get married in the park. I've got to go pick up my tuxedo."

That was a lie. Our faux wedding ceremony wasn't until the following week, but I needed to say something!

I would rather do literally nothing than actually work out. But, it really bothered me that I was letting this guy down.

One day I decided I couldn't live like that anymore. I had to make a change! And I did.
The very next day, I started walking a different way to get home. I avoided the street the gym was on entirely!

It's been a few weeks now and I haven't seen that guy. I'm hoping he thinks I'm dead.

That's where I am in life. Someone thinking I'm dead is actually better than him knowing the truth about how unmotivated I am. At least I can fake die with some dignity. But alive, I'm just a lazy slacker with a body as soft and tender as a piece of veal in pudding form.

Chapter 17
THE SPORTSCASTER WHO DOESN'T KNOW ANYTHING ABOUT SPORTS

Hello everyone, and welcome to another exciting game of sports! I'm Bob Sportsman. Thank you for joining us.

We've got a great one for you tonight. There are a lot of die-hard fans who came out to this one. But let's not forget that without the players on the teams, these sports fans would have very little to see. It would pretty much just be a big empty field, or stadium, or court, or whatever.

Both of these teams really want to win, and the fans have their particular preferences as to which of these teams they are rooting for, but it's my understanding that only one team will leave the victor. The other will undoubtedly leave defeated.

If it were possible for both of these teams to win, this game would just not be as exciting to watch.

Let's talk about the stats of these two teams. Both teams have won some games before, but they've also both lost before. So, for my money, I'm going to say the team with the most amount of points at the end of this thing, is the team that will be declared the winner.

If neither of these teams here win this thing tonight, I'd be very surprised, and it surely would be one for the history books, indeed.

I'm pretty sure that both of these teams did a little bit of practicing before tonight, just to make sure they were ready to play the actual game. And boy, oh boy is it paying off! Some of these plays are being executed in such a way, that I'm pretty sure they were at least discussed beforehand.

What's this? It appears they have started posting the point system on some sort of board. A scoreboard, if you will. That's really going to help avoid some confusion later on in the game. The fans have definitely got to be happy about that.

At the beginning of the game, both teams had zero points, and they have been working their way up from there. And I have to say; it's really going to be interesting to see how this whole thing plays out.

The thing to remember is that I don't believe any of these players have day jobs. They are all full-time, professional athletes. And they certainly are "athlete-ing" it up all over the place right now. These fans are absolutely loving it.

I am pretty sure the fans have day jobs, though. I'm not sure, but I don't think they get paid to follow their particular favorite teams.
That being said, these fans are not part-time fans. They are full time. If the fans here tonight were employed by

these teams, they would definitely qualify for health benefits, and a 401K. I'm talking full retirement plan.

These fans are putting on quite a display tonight! It almost feels like it's their job. They are in the business of loving sports, and business is good.

The MVP tonight is definitely going to be the player who is the most valuable to the other teammates during the course of this game. And you can quote me on that.

Well, after a grueling display of athletics, finally one of these talented teams of athletes has defeated the other. We have a winner, and the crowd is going nuts!

Half of the crowd is happy, and the other half is beside themselves with rage, anger, and disappointment. Needless to say, there are a great deal of emotions being felt here tonight.

Thank you for tuning in at home and watching sports. I'm Bob Sportsman. We will see you next time sports are played. And remember, life is a game of sports. Play hard! Goodnight!

Chapter 18
CLOSING

Well, it looks as though we have come to the end of the book. I hope you had as much fun reading it as I had writing it. Actually, I hope you had way more fun than I did.

Writing a book is a lot of work. Plus, I had to draw all those pictures. Man, what a waste of time. I could have been doing so many other things.

Oh well. You live you learn. Wait, what did I learn? What did you learn?! Did any of us learn anything? Probably not. But perhaps you had a few laughs while flipping through the pages of my very first book. Maybe you will even read my second book, if I decide to write one.

Did you have a good time? The question was rhetorical, though I do hope the answer is, "The book was great, Anthony! Thanks for asking!"

If the answer is, "Fuck you, Anthony! I hate this book," then please, keep it to yourself. That criticism is not very constructive, and my answer to you would be, "Well is your book any better?"

If you have, in fact, written a better book, I would

apologize for being so rude to you. Congratulations on your book, and all of the success you have achieved! You were right to speak up about my inferiority.

If you have not written a book, then I stand by what I said, unless you are really intimidating. I don't want any trouble here. I just wanted to write a book that was mildly humorous. Just leave me alone, you big bully! What are you trying to prove?

Thanks for making it to the very end of my book! You are really cool. How will you know when the book is over? It will say, "The end." Wait for it...almost...it won't be long now...I think I can hear it coming. I smell it too. That's sort of strange...Well, that's all for me. Bye!

The end.

ABOUT THE AUTHOR

Didn't I do this shit already?

Okay, let me get back into third person narrative. This should sound professional.

Anthony Kapfer is a comedian, musician, filmmaker, cartoonist, animator, actor, author, and narcissist.

Anthony was born in New York City, and is the only person in the history of the entire world (probably) to have lived in all five boroughs, (Yes, even Staten Island).

Anthony shares a birthday with legendary film director, Alfred Hitchcock (different year of birth).

Anthony's parents considered naming him Dylan at one point. They also considered, Wolfgang as another option. Anthony thinks either of those names would have been a better choice than Anthony.

Anthony Kapfer's comedy and music has been featured in various TV shows, films, radio, blah blah blah…

Anthony Kapfer hopes you enjoyed reading this book, and he sincerely thanks you for buying it. You're the best!